OLD
Family
NEW
Enemies

Aileen Read

authorHOUSE®

AuthorHouse™
1663 Liberty Drive
Bloomington, IN 47403
www.authorhouse.com
Phone: 1 (800) 839-8640

Published by AuthorHouse 08/17/2018

ISBN: 978-1-5462-5581-9 (sc)
ISBN: 978-1-5462-5580-2 (e)

Library of Congress Control Number: 2018909789

DEDICATION

To my true family In Germany, North Carolina, and DC, my two best friends who have proven to be my sisters, and my two daughters. I love you all dearly!

YOU CAN CHOOSE YOUR FRIENDS BUT NOT YOUR FAMILY

This story will make you think over and over about trusting family. after dealing with some family members financially and some showing Ill-willed towards me ...I come to believe that we are not as close-knit or trustworthy as I thought. and that some of them have a lot of hate and jealousy for each other. since mommy died… there really Isn't any meaning to the word family at least not with us. when mommy was alive we made time for her and each other, now I do believe It's only because she was alive... and we were all younger. there are so many of us I could hardly keep up with, now that we are older and a couple of my siblings are deceased, I tried to keep up with most of them 'but now I don't want or care to. I have no need for most of their company. It's to much drama, and wasted time energy & money. especially when I spend $3000 to $5000 every year for the family gatherings ...thanks ungrateful... and I mean this to most of them that my poor mother gave birth to. I don't have to feed you ungrateful people anymore. I can now save my money for my grandchildren. my sisters and brothers most of them are my worst enemies. they didn't know how to appreciate when they had something good, because they never had anyone to teach them, I tried but they were already set In their own ways. with the little time that they lived with me I think I did a good job trying to teach them how to appreciate others. when someone does something for them that they didn't have to do, I think I did a good job. I should say I wasn't good I was great…because when mommy died I kept those ungrateful out of foster care...no other family members wanted all those kids, when mommy died she still had 6 children left for me to care for. If you ever had people related to you like this ...you could really lose your mind. the old saying... you can choose your friends....but you can't choose your family... it's not true with me...i have chosen my own family and not to be Involved with most of the ones that came from my mother. sorry mom but you gave birth to some evil children and I'm so glad you are not here to experience their bulshit. I say to myself quite often... If I gave them so much love and care ...and they kick me while down... I can only Imagine what would they have done to my mother? I never would have thought things could be so bad between us siblings on mommy side of the family. makes me wish I was the only child. thank god for the sisters and brothers on my dad side and my 4 male cousins from my dad side and my auntie and seven girl cousins from auntie side, and a couple of great cousin they are the most wonderful people In my life. Im always looking forward to seeing them when I take my vacations. I will choose my family, I will stay away from my mother's side... as far as possible. I know now people change some In the worst way as adults... Including some In my family. some change for the better not these folks. and a lot of them have no morals and some become dogs and bite the hand that fed them. It's so sad that I feel like this... like a stupid person who cares about family members...they didn't give a damn about me. the sibling that I was closest to, was jr he hurt me so bad...he sent so much pain to my chest that I can't even describe. I don't know If I hurt him as much as he hurt me I didn't think so...but I do know this pain Is still with me and Its been over 5 years now. some people say they believe I hurt him more but I still don't think so. I talked about his actions to the family members...but I had to, I needed to talk to them because he robbed me blind and for a lot of money... I never seen this coming. I told one of our other siblings that I thought jr was acting strange. was he ashamed that I ask family members about his weird behavior? that only happen because when I talk to him about the house or anything to do with the money he owed me, he talk very nasty to me. It didn't make any sense talking to him mostly because he's always stone. I thought he would pay me the money he owed me, but he just lived In my house like a squatter. maybe I should have ask him direct In his face what Is going on with him and those young boys living In my house, with him & them freeloading on my expense. he's not paying bills or rent because he said he's waiting for a retroactive payment from his disability case and I believed him, I did not throw him out of my house I felt sorry for him. but there Is much more to this story, I cannot put him out because I'm not nasty and mean like him. he also knows I will not put him out because he was the closest sibling to me for over 40 years. but I know now that I was not his favorite person because those young boys meant so much to him. he's throwing out my children who pays the bills for him & those young boys who pays for nothing. who the hell are these young boys and where are their parents? I do not care about what you do with your adult male companions but when It comes to young children 18 years and younger you have to explain what you are doing with these children. did these parents know their children was hanging out with this 50 year old weirdo? I never seen any women coming from his apartment ever, only a bunch of old drunk men or young boys with red eyes and smelling like weed. and the neighbors confirm It too. he was telling family members that those boys did a lot for him. I want to know what did they do? we paid the mortgage, the water bill & gas & electric & carfare to the your doctor, so what the hell did those boys do for him? I really want to know? when my husband cheated on me with his co-worker I gave him an ultimatum after so many years of dealing with his cheating ways he wanted to come back home, so I said If you want to come back home you have to sign the business property over to me and my brother... he agreed to do so. what a big mistake I made In trusting my brother more than my husband. I was trying to protect my assets and make sure my husband didn't take my Invested money and give It to his bitch... she had nothing and wanted everything I had. and I was also looking out for my brother who never had anything... he was living In a one room basement apartment paying $800, I ask him to move In my four room apartment for $500... he was very happy to move In my house. he was so happy that he gave me a extra $100 dollars. he went through a nasty divorce, and he said his ex-wife took all his money and left him with nothing. and his son didn't have anything to do with him, I was dumb because I felt sorry for jr. he told me all kind of crazy stories and I believed him. he made me believe the ex-wife stole all his savings and he told me he found her In his bed with her female co-worker and another time he found her sleeping with her nephew from previous marriage. than he told me his son stole a lot of money from him, than I found out the son wasn't going to college and told us he was... my brother and I were giving this kid money for school. I stayed away from the ex-wife and the son...once upon a time they were my favorite sister In law and nephew, my brother ruined that too. but the ex-wife called me one day to ask me what Is going on with my brother her x her sons father? because as soon as child support was over with his son he never had anything to do with his son ever again...and It's been 10 years and more. but I know for sure It had nothing to do with his ex-wife or son. he just didn't want his son to know he Is living with these young boys and doing lots of drugs. my brother started his drug habit all over again...just like he did In the early 80s, and I know because my older son told me his friend sold my brother cocaine. I knew when my brother was working he stayed high and broke. I always wanted to know why he alway stayed away from all of the sisters and brothers and his only child. this time around now I'm getting the bad treatment. he thinks I cannot see what's going on at the other house but the neighbors are very nosey In that area and I love It because even though I'm not there they call me and tell me everything. one time one of the neighbors called me asking me to come over to check and see If jr was ok... I ask her why would you think something happen to my brother... she reply that she was worried because she seen him hanging out with a bunch of strange looking young boys. I went to check on him and he open the door smelling like weed & alcohol. I ask him If he was ok? he reply why the fuck do you care about me? I was so shock I left and never returned. I know this last argument started because of Dan, we had a family reunion and Dan could not make It because he could not get anyone to keep his children. you see he has disabled children and It's very hard for his wife to handle them alone. but for him to have special need children he made time to stay In the family bulshit, I do not know how Dan had so much time on his hand with special need children, but he was always In a lot of family drammer with jr. I think his wife Is so sweet but so blind Dan has a problem with cheating on his wife. I know this for a fact because he went to my brother Sam's wedding and slept with an old friend of my new sister In law. my brother Sam was upset because he didn't want his new wife to think he's a dog like his brother Dan. Sam's wife told him not to hang out with his brother Dan because she didn't trust

Dan, and she's right to not trust him. and Dan was telling everyone of us that he didn't like Sam's wife. and I didn't know why he said this. I heard that Sam pulled a gun on Dan to stay away from his house, Dan didn't know that Sam really hated him until Sam pulled a gun out on him, during a heated argument between the two of them. but that hate between the two of them goes way back when they were little boys Sam always beat Dan ass because Dan was a troublemaker just like he Is now as an adult. but now I see why he said this... Its because he jealous of Sam and his wife. Dan Is a low life dog just like his junkie father was to my mother. Dan and jr are very close now and I do not care for either one of them. I think Dan was upset with me staying away from him due to him being a troublemaker In the family. so he showed jr how to hurt me, and I know for a fact Dan and Tina are so bitter In their own lives... they walked the junkie brother jr through how to steal my house. and It worked... they did steal It from me and my husband and children but I will have my day In court. I think they are good with each other because they dog women and no one In the family likes either one of them, and Its because they were no good to their own mother. jr supply my mother with lots of Illegal pills which helped slowly deteriorate her life...she was dying slowly, she was a pill addict for a long time with my grandmother, but jr worked In a pharmacy and had easy access to supply mommy with most of those drugs. I think he knows he help kill our mother and that's why he's screwed up In the head and on drugs still today. he doesn't care about anyone because he knows he participated In killing his mother. our sister Diana helped too because she let our mother die In that fire. I know for a fact they have bad luck because they didn't give a dam for their own mother and Dan too, the morning before she died she told me she will never forgive Dan for hitting her while she was In that wheelchair. she died and never forgave him. i hope he feels like shit for the rest of his life. when mommy died I took care of him and those careless ungrateful. jr gave her an electric bed which she died In and I think jr knew that bed was a defect. his conscience Is eating him up and thats why hes still on drugs, he will not admit to having some responsibility In that defected bed he gave mommy. and Dan had treated mommy horribly too, he hit her and she put his ass away In a all boys home when he was about 16 years old. jr and Dan and Sofia and Diana are all troublemakers they talk negative about everybody because they are very bitter about their childhood. they don't like to see others happy. they have a lot of skeletons In their closet. Dan could not come to the reunion so he started an argument between jr and me. It was not a family secret, but Dan told jr he talk to another sibling and that was Carlos... he said my father told him that he Is not jr father. we heard about this...that me / jr /sofia / sam... may not be my fathers children. my dad always said we were not his children...and that It's possible we are his brothers children... uncle henry. my dad never took a dna test to prove we were not his children...so I always thought he was talking shit because he was mad at my mother. and he was trying to keep my stepmother from knowing he was with the two of them at the Same time. I think Dan Is a very jealous person because his father was a junkie, and my father took very good care of us even though my father didn't give a damn about my mother. Dan always talking like he was better than anyone of us and he's alway competing with one of us. I watched him always In competition with children In school and always with family members and co-workers. If you have a car he will tell you In your face... I'm going to get a bigger & better car, he did this to me when I bought my first house, he said to me why did you buy this little house? I told him me and my family are happy and this Is what I can afford. he did go and buy a much bigger house and he also bought a couple of business properties and lost them because he got greedy...just to show off. and also he slept with all of his tenants. Dan was a smart boy growing up, but as he got older he started to become a womanizer and arrogant and boasting about every women he had and dogged. his wife made lots of money but he used her and made her bankrupt...just cause he has to show off. I know he talked to my family about all the dirt my husband did to me but my brothers and sisters told me about him too. he was so horrible to women, so much so that his twin use to get beat up for him... mistaken Identity Is bad when you have an evil twin. as he got older he start talking a lot of dirty shit about everyone In the family like he hates all of them... especially the sisters. when I was the only one In the family that kept In touch with him he would tell me how he hated all of our siblings and I think he knew they hated him too...because he treated our mother so bad. and jr act like he love mommy so much but he gave her all those drugs. when she died jr was telling all the family that he wanted to kill himself, I guess he knew In many ways he was responsible for her death. first for giving her all those pills to make her too weak to get out of that burning bed. Dan has no real life happiness so he gets on the phone with anyone of the family that would listen to him. and stirs up a bunch of lies to start fights with each other, Dan and jr really get a kick out making people miserable because they are so unhappy and they both need lots of attention. jr and Dan are weak without each other.

IF I WOULD HAVE KNOWN

If I knew my mother's father a little longer, than I probably would have been able to know mommy family tree better. my mother use to say that I remind her of her mother, and my sisters and brothers all said I was crazy like her. Mommy was crazy and that shows me why everyone else thinks I'm crazy just like her. But I don't know where the evil side of my mother's children came from. I knew grandpa was a kind man, but him and my mother did not have a good relationship, because of her and her husband's drug problem no one want to be bother with them. I remembered my mother going to see her father and her auntie a couple of times. she love her father's sister so much she always talk about her. And then she stopped keeping In touch with them. and I ask my mother why did she stop going to see her father? She said her father didn't like her husband and I knew why. My mother gave up her relationship with her father and auntie and brothers for her husband and that I will never understand why. My grandfather was a very Interesting person and my uncle's was too. I talk to my grandfather on the phone when my mother was alive, but he never said much but hello and hope to meet all her kids, I guess at the time we were not able to meet him because It was too many of us. and mommy could not afford to take one of us let alone ten of us to visit her father. I didn't meet my grandfather until my mother died. I called my grandfather to tell him about my mother's death. He said he was so sorry that he didn't get to see her. But I told him I know she loved him very much, cause she always told me she loves her father. And then he told me not to do like she did by staying away. I told him that I promise I will make sure he meet all mama's children. And that I did. Once I got my next vacation I took the first one jr to meet grandpa. The first think grandpa said was jr Is crazy, and that's for sure... and then I brought his wife to meet grandpa and the first thing he said Is she's crazy too. grandpa was good at judging a person's character. Grandpa always made me laugh when the three of us use to come to see him. He always joked about the relationship between jr and Emma. I know they were crazy when grandpa said It. Than we brought their son to meet grandpa, he said he felt sorry for The little boy. He said they drove the kid crazy and that was so true they argued In front of that kid all the time. Than I brought Sofia and Diana and Karen to meet him. he didn't say much about them because It was a short visit and only twice, those three came and they were hard to convince to come see him. because Susan didn't want to meet him the other sisters said they didn't like the Idea that he didn't have anything to do with mommy his own daughter. I explain to them that mommy had a pill addiction and he didn't want to give her money for drugs. then they understood. when they met him they start to tell the other brothers how much he was like his daughter, so now they start to make plans to go see him. but he got sick and wanted to come live with me so I made plans for him to come live with me. that's the time the brothers came to meet him and they start to like him and they visit him at my house more often. than grandpa got home sick. and he wanted to go back to Washington. so I drove him back and then started to visit him every three months. then I start to really get to know my grandpa he told me some great stories about his childhood. he told me his mother was a twin and we never knew this because we didn't know his mother. and we always wanted to know where the twins came from because mom had twins. and he told me he didn't know his mother either because she died from giving birth to him, because he was a 12 pound baby boy. and that's another thing mommy didn't tell us. and he also told me he was 12 or 13 years old when he ran away from his auntie, and he told me he crossed the Mississippi River and got a job In a bar selling alcohol. He said he was so big that no one knew he was only 13 years old, he said they thought he was 18 and that's why they let him work In the bars. He told me that he loved jazz. That's one thing we had In common, he also told me that he use to know Louis Armstrong and Ella Fitzgerald dizzy Gillespie. I was so amazed to hear my grandpa knew these famous people. And he worked as a head chef In the white house when Nixon was president. He had his

9

one daughter from his first wife and that was my mother, She died, than he had a son from his second wife and he died, mommy knew him but we never got the chance to meet him. than grandpa got married a third time and had another son. And that son turned out to be his best child he had. He work as an special government agent. And grandpa was so proud of him. My mother didn't spend much time with him. But at least she met him. I like my uncle he's a very smart man. I met his mother she was a smart women. she was my grandpa 3rd wife and she was always making jokes about her marriage to my grandpa. They had a good friendship after their divorce. My mother was his only daughter so before he died he told me that he want to repay me for being the only child my mother had that came to help take care of him. I told him the only thing I wanted was his sister dolls and he agreed that I would Inherited them when he die. But my uncle never gave them to me. And I'm still waiting for my grandpa sisters babies and all three of them. Well I can say I don't know where the evil side of my brother and sisters came from.

NO BROTHERLY - LOVE

when I put together the familyreunion...not In a million years would I believe that this was going to be the end of my relationship with most of my family. Im sooooooo surprised to find out after the reunion that so many of my brothers and sisters hated each other. and now I my self hate a lot of them too. and I do mean a lot of them from my mother. I had the reunion In my backyard and out of the ten children from mommy nine of them came. the only one missing was Dan... the evil twin. It might as well have been a boxing match...because everyone was mad at each other... except me. jr didn't like Stan because he ask him to lend him a ladder 5 years ago and Stan never came with the ladder so they didn't talk for years and not much at the reunion. for years I told jr to stop being mad at Stan for a dam ladder but jr hated everybody except me at least not yet. nor did jr like Carlos either and this goes way back... from when they were 10 and 12 years old and they are 50 year old men now and hate each other bad... Carlos Is the oldest boy from mommy so he would beat up jr and boss him around. jr always cried to me about Carlos being mean to him... jr never liked him... as a matter of a fact he hates Carlos. when It was just the 3 of us jr always stayed with me. jr said he hated Carlos more when he got older because jr did everything for mommy and Carlos gave my mother & father hell. jr said he went to take mommy shopping one day and he put mommy In the car and the car would not start. jr told me he open the hood and the radiator was missing. jr told me that he knew for a fact that Carlos stole the radiator. I ask him was he sure? he said that he had a couple of witnesses In mommys building that seen him take the radiator out of jr car and put It In his car. I always wanted to ask Carlos If he did that to jr but I left that argument alone. then jr and Carlos never had too much to do with each other still until the time when mommy died. jr and I was sitting In the house trying to get the funeral preparations going, when we got a phone call from the renting office of mommy's building and the clerk said to me... ms Judy your brother Carlos ask for the keys to enter your mother's apartment and I said ok thats not a problem. jr got suspicious about Carlos going there and he ran over to the apartment to see what did Carlos take, jr came back and told me that Carlos took all of mommy's jewelry and I don't know how true this was because I could not go Into that apartment where my mother died. but that wasn't the end of the chaos between them more happened when Carlos tried to stop me and jr from claiming mommy's body from the morgue. Carlos called the morgue and told them that he's the oldest child and he wants mommy's body, i ask him why was he doing this to us? he didn't have to tell me I knew why... It's because when mommy died he came to my house after not seeing us for more than 2 or 3 years and his first born child was there with his mom. and my brother Carlos start to tell me he didn't want them there. and I told him If he didn't like his son and his sons mother being there In my house he Is more than welcome to leave...and he did leave my house pissed off at me. so that's why me and Carlos had It out for each other and that's why he tried to take mommy's body from us. now when he called the mogue I ask him where was he and he said he was at the funeral home... I went straight there to take his eyes out of his head, and his wife call the police on me, when the police arrive they ask us what happen and why are we fighting over my mother's body? I told the officer that my brother Carlos didn't have any money so he wants to put my mother In potters field and we told him we have the money to have a decent burial for my mother. the officers told Carlos to sign an affidavit to give me and jr permission to retrieve mommy's body and me and my husband gave my mother a great burial with no problem. jr and Carlos never had anything to do with each other since that day. but I started a tradition In the family to get all of us together every year for mothers day to remember our mother. and for a long time the event turned out nice. one day after 15 years passed Carlos came to me asking me to forgive him about the time at the funeral home. and I told him that I will forgive him because we never had any problems before that or after... even until today. so I Invited him to our mother's day cookout.

15 years later jr was still angry at Carlos and jr was angry at me for Inviting our oldest brother to my gathering. so the fight started at the cemetery, we all went to the cemetery and Carlos came to the cemetery and jr and Dan start to scream at Carlos... they said what the hell are you doing here? Carlos said I came to join you all and visit my mother's grave site. Stan ask Carlos who told you mommy was buried here? Carlos answer... Judy told me, they all looked at me like they wanted to kill me and then they all started to fight right on my mother's grave. I scream at them saying get off of my mothers grave and stop this bulshit fighting. he Is our brother so forgive him and they did. and after that we didn't see Carlos until this family reunion again as usual at my house and at my expense every year. this was the biggest fight that will be the talk of all our life. and all because of jr and Dan. the 2 most chaotic children mommy ever had. jr always hated Carlos...and this time he didn't hide It. when we all sat at the table In the backyard I could hear jr making sarcastic remarks. he said look at Carlos and Judy...now they are buddy buddy and than he started more sarcastic remark when I said to Sam come say hello to your father jr scream you mean your father and papa said what did jr say? I said to papa don't pay attention to jr, he Is drunk or high as usual. after we all start to talk to papa, jr was walking around saying strange things to different family members and they just laugh at him. no one understood him, he always got drunk and high and start to talk nonsense. then I see Stan and Susan trying to clear up the argument they had over 20 years ago. Stan told Susan that he had found a nice apartment that they could share. Susan gave him a couple hundred dollars and Stan took the money and never got the apartment. and did something else with the money, and Susan never saw Stan again after that for about 5 years. Susan called Stan and curse him out and they didn't speak for over 20 years. now at the reunion they are In the corner of my yard and Stan Is begging for Susan to forgive him. but Susan Is looking In the opposite direction like she doesn't give a damn about his apology. and If I know my sister Susan she still not talking to Stan. now Stan leaves the corner of the house and goes to the front yard to try and apologize to our sister Diana. and the argument started with Stan telling Diana to grow up and be a more responsible person and stop having children without getting married. that was It Diana told him to mine his business. and then Stan tried to get Diana to go to his church to

ask god to forgive her but Diana refused and she didn't talk to Stan for a couple of years. and now he's begging for her to forgive him. I do not know If they talk to each other because after that day I never talk to neither one of them. jr told Stan that I hated him because he stole mommy's jewelry I knew from that moment jr was trying to make family members hate me because we all know that jr said Carlos stole mommy's jewelry. now Stan moved through the back yard to try to make peace with Sam you see what happen to him and Stan was because Stan doesn't want anyone of his family members In his house. so one day Sam went to Stan house and didn't Invite Sam In, he told Sam to wait outside, when Stan came outside he said I'm sorry I can't let you In the house because my wife Is sleeping, Sam told him that It was ok and he never had anything to do with Stan again. back to the reunion Stan stood In the middle of my yard looking like a lost dog. now he went to our sister Karen telling her that he's sorry he never comes by to see her, she so humble she just accepts his apology and never has anything to do with him after that. Karen and Stan never had too much to say to each other because Stan always preaching sermons from the bible and Karen doesn't care about religion. now Stan goes to Carlos to try to get to know him now, these are the funniest two siblings to ever get together because Carlos doesn't even know Stan's name. yep you see mommy had so many kids that the last 5 Carlos could never remember their names. Stan Is a twin to Dan and Carlos always ask me what were their names? and I would always laugh at this because now Carlos asks Stan which twin are you? With Stan not having a good relationship with Carlos & jr & Sofia & Sam & Diana & Karen especially Susan.... that reunion was a lot of tension In the yard that day. and I was thanking GOD that his twin Dan was not able to be there. I know for a fact everyone has a lot of hate for those twins. they cause so much chaos together that If they were there together somebody would have been shot or In jail. now jr and Carlos was my biggest worry but they didn't turn out to be the biggest problem. the problem turned out to be Susan and Sofia. because Susan moved out of state and left her apartment to Sofia and Sofia stop paying the rent. now Susan and Sofia are as thick as thieves nothing can come between those two not even Sofia owing Susan money. Susan must have a special love for Sofia because when Stan owed Susan money she didn't have nothing to do with him for more than 20 years and still

till this day. and he only owed her $200 but Sofia owed her $8000, I know for a fact that Susan wanted to beat the hell out of Sofia 2 daughters because those bitches and whores stayed In that apartment with their mother and there men and never paid the rent. I knew those trashy bitches would do that to Susan and Its good for her she knows our sister Sofia reputation. Sofia did the Same thing to jr...him and his wife just got married so he move out of his apartment and moved In with his wife, jr and his wife wanted to buy a house they went to do a credit check and whamm... that hit jr smack In the face Sofia didn't pay the rent. jr and his wife had to throw her ass out and pay the back rent... she left jr paying $10,000 for back rent and she was living there with one of her hundred boy friends. and she did It to him again jr opened a salon and went In partnership with Sofia and Sam...sofia was robbing them blind she never took the money to the night deposit and she had cell phone and credit cards from the business In her name and went on a spending spree, she owe them $15,000 to $ 20,000. now after years of her stealing from most of her brothers and sisters, she gets the gold medal for best sister ever and most respected...everyone says poor little Sofia and now more because she's sick. I did nothing wrong to any of them and owed not one of them anything and took nothing from them...but I get the kick In the ass. i know Susan respects and love her because she babysat for her and Diana's children, but I kept them out of foster care when both their parents died. and I gave them a lot of great times to remember. I never knew why Sofia Is always sick... because she's alway been so secretive and sneaky. and she has two daughters just like her, they are sneaky liars and thieves, those bitches...I never want anything to do with them....now the oldest one Is much worse than her mother she went to prison for witnessing one boy friend kill the other. why would someone kill anyone for her I never understood that one...because she's not a nice person at all. she's a con-artist & a slick thief she will rob you blind while talking slick shit to you...her hand will be In your pocket and you will never see It coming. I remember going In a store with her and a bunch of other family members and we all looked at her, she was laughing coming out the of store. we ask why are you laughing she said because Im wearing a new coat and sunglasses...we ask her how did she get the coat and sunglasses? you see she went In the store without a coat and glasses on and walk right out the store with a new one on without paying for the coat or glasses. I told her I would never go anywhere with her ever again, until this day I have never been anywhere with those thieves. later that day I found her sister betty stole a pair of shoes that cost $5 and that bitch had a job making $35,000 a year. but you know-how those two thieves can not have anything good because they follow their mother stealing from anyone and everyone.

BLOOD-RELATIVES

the reason why they dont have shit Is because their mother taught them how to steal from any and everyone they can... even from family members. I remember Tina stole a $5 disposable camera from me and she swore In my face that she didn't do It and then I saw my pictures on her computer, I ask her how did she get those pictures? she said someone gave them to her, the pictures were of my 25th anniversary In my house. she must have thrown mine and my husband and other family member pictures In the garbage. because I only saw pictures of her In my house from that day. and I know for a fact because I snapshot those pictures. that happen to me because I knew she's a thief and I should have kept them out of my house. that's the way they have been with everyone In the family, no one trust Sofia and her 2 thieves. I can tell you there's a lot of the brothers homes Sofia and her children never been In, the sisters have nothing much for them to take. I find It to be such a coincidence that Sofia didn't pay rent In jr apartment and left him and his new wife Emma with a bill from the salon and the apartment totaling $30,000 and just at the time of jr and Emma getting married and trying to buy a new home. and she did the Same thing to Susan at the Same time when she was getting married too. and owed Susan and her new husband $8000 or more. I find that you all love Sofia and her bulshit so much. since I thought about how I did nothing to hurt you all never took any money or anything from you all I come to the conclusion to never ever have anything to do with you all again till the day I die. I made the family reunion happen for all those years that we missed with each other. and I can guarantee there will never ever be another. some of these sisters and brothers have so much bulshit going on In their lives. I don't know how they find time to make problems with each other. I don't call these screwed up family members until I have a bbq because I have two jobs and no time for bulshit. I get together with them mothers day and thanksgiving and the whole year I don't have any time for myself let alone them. and most of them are argumentative like the twins I hate talking to them because they think they know It all and jr Is very bossy he talks to me like I'm his slave, when he calls me he says come over here and pick up the rent then he gives me a list of orders no matter what time or day It Is. and he talks to me like I owe him something when he's living In my house. and when I'm sick he never ask me how am I feeling he just talk down at me like he's angry at the world so he takes It out on me. I was very close to him once upon a time ...never ever again. I hardly ever hear from Carlos and of lately we get along better than any of my mother's children. Sofia never had any time for me, she loves Susan. I would see her and those bitch daughters of hers only at bbqs and they would steal any and everything they can carry. she never had much to say to me so I can say for a fact she never act like a sister to me and Susan I never had a real sister hood with her neither she calls me once every 2 or 3 years to see If I'm still alive I guess. and Diana Same like Sofia & Susan all three are thick as thieves. I don't think they ever liked me. I always had special love for Karen because she's always calling me to ask how am I doing? and vice versa. I can cry right now because she was 7 years old when mommy died and 4 years old when her father died, she never had much of a mother or father. she's very kind to people like mommy was. I feel so sorry for Karen because the sisters and brothers all treat her like shit as a matter of fact they treat her just like they treat me. we are the forgotten ones, and I'm the oldest girl and she's the baby girl maybe that's why we were so close...once upon a time. I'm a little disappointed with her right now because she went back to Diana and spread a lot of unnecessary gossip, and my daughter went away and left her to care for my grandbaby and she didn't do a good job. I don't care to much about the gossip but she did not know that the gossip she spread cause a argument between my son and dumbass sister Diana and jr and Dan. now Sam we were once very close, I was very surprise when he called and told me to make my children leave my house that I'm paying for, why should I give up my house that I paid for...to give the jackass jr a peace of mind, If jr was paying his rent, we would not have a problem right now. so I think Sam should not have got Involved thats why Im not speaking to Sam right now. and jr, Dan, Stan, sofia, Diana, Karen, Susan, Tina, betty 8 sisters and brothers and 2 niece till today, all of you are the third party In the order of protection so If you want to know why I'm not talking to you...ask your fucked up brother jr. you all know what you did to me was not right, I think they all know... do not expect to hear from me again ever In life. most of you go through life with your eyes closed and can't tell the difference between a liar and a thief they are the Same person. If you see something that makes no sense you should walk the other way and take another direction, but no you walk right Into the bulshit the liars & thieves handed you. jr and Sam and Susan was robbed by Sofia but they choose to live with those trouble making people...not me. and now jr and Sofia and Tina and betty robbed me I will not live with these kind of people just because my mother and my sister gave birth to them.

OLD FAMILY NEW ENEMIES

as time goes by I do not like my so-call family that I thought meant so much to me. I cannot remember my enemies doing me this dirty. Standing In family court with my so-call favorite brother making false allegations against me and my family knocked me off my feet. the first time I entered the courtroom I had a blackout for 5 minutes, I still don't know how I kept Standing. all I can remember was hearing the judge reading the charges and I'm looking at him with so much hate, saying to myself what a liar…I hardly know this person that I helped raise. I couldn't do these low life things to people, It's never been my character Im a very kind and caring person but bossy, it's my way most of the time …the sisters and brothers obeyed me because my mother always made me In charge of the house & siblings. she trusted me and I got shit done starting at the age of 8 years old. I think the siblings got tired of me as we got older because the younger ones start to disrespect me. Carlos was the oldest…he was always gone, he had a unicycle and he was great at riding that one wheel bike. I was always showing him off to my friends. and he had lots of friends so he was never around the house much… and mommy was always out looking for him. he would steal mommys money and disappear all day. than she would call my father to beat him for not taking out the garbage or not doing the dishes or not walking the dog, and stealing from her. but I would always be the one to tell on him so when he came back home he would beat me up for squealing. I took Carlos clunks on my head like a champ but not jr… It was a war when Carlos clunked jr. Carlos never wanted to do errands… sometimes he gave me candy and money to do them so mommy didn't beat his butt. my great grandmother loved him so much she would always stop my father from whipping his behind. she would always tell him to go outside to get away from my father. that boy love being outside I didn't know much about Carlos but I know he loved being outside away from us and mommy and he didn't like mommy. I knew he was always mad at mommy I think because he saw her with my uncle and other men other than my father. Carlos and I and jr would go with my father on trips and Carlos would stay very tight lip about my father's brother uncle henry coming over. and jr and I would always say hello to my uncle and we would go outside to play, but I notice my brother would stay In the house when my uncle came by. I know now why my brother Carlos stayed In the house then. to watch him with my mom, he hated my uncle henry so bad...and now I know why. Carlos would push me to be strong and never give up on making things work. he didn't want me to be weak like my mother. he really pushed me to be tough and strong and I thank him for pushing me to be strong. he taught me how to ride a bike and ride the back of moving trucks. and he taught me how to be as strong as wonder woman and evil knievel. that's why I can deal with a lot of shit today as a grown women. just like evil knievel did crazy stunts my brother Carlos did as many crazy stunts too and I followed because I was a tomboy and I love doing daring stunts with my brother Carlos. I was In the middle of two boys...one was really tough Carlos and the other jr was soft as a girl. as we got older Carlos still stays away ....i think he's smart and he plays It safe staying away from these crazy family members... because he stays away he has less problems with the family ... hey Carlos I'm starting to think and do just like you Im staying far away from this crazy family. as he grow older he had a lot of children just like my mother, and he finally settle down and married a wonderful women Natasha. after all the crazy girlfriends he had. and all those children like my mother. two things I pray my brother Carlos would do... #1 I pray for him to forgive my mother for all of the mistake she made with us. I know she tried so hard to take care of us the best way she knew how... god knows she had a lot of us. and #2 please keep good communication with all of your children so they would never have to go though what you went through with our parents. now my brother jr he never wanted to do anything In his childhood he would always walk behind me. and I think It was because he had crossed eyes and the other kids would tease and laugh at him. but as long as he stay close to me he felt safe because he knew I wouldn't let anyone pick with him. that's how we became so close. as I sit back and think about It...he didn't have any friends, and never had a hobby. he was very shy because of the crossed eyes. and he cried to me for every little thing just like he does now...and always cried to me not to mommy or daddy. I was call to his classes all the time because someone would pick with him In school. and the teachers would call me out of my class just to calm him down. he would be holding a chair up In the air threatening to hit someone over their head for bothering him. I seen jr get easily agitated when Carlos would pick with him. when I think about It now I see his character very shy and didn't trust anyone but me and mommy. he didn't even like our father, I remember my father always telling him to speak up and my father always ask me If something was wrong with him? and he would start to cry but he would act bold and hold It In so my father would stop lecturing him. and sometimes he stay home with mommy because he hated my father or just didn't want to be around him or my stepmother. I don't know If he hated our father because he couldn't take daddy criticizing him or because daddy denied us to other people but daddy never said It to his face. now that I see him as an adult he Is the total opposite of when he was a child. he's not anything near shy and he's loud and disrespectful to women and especially to me. I feel like I don't even know him anymore he's always high and loud and obnoxious and so negative. when he talks to me I just want to run far from him. I remembered when he was 15 years old working In the drug store he start to change, and I know for a fact It's because he had a girl that was twice his age. and she act like she was his mother...i guess that's what he was looking for a mother Image. and she was a hard core junkie, I think she turned him on to those drugs. the both of them worked In the drugstore and him and her both stole drugs from there. and that's how mommy got her drugs too, I know now why jr was her favorite child, It's very clear to me now. as he got older you never knew what was his next move... he was never home and he would always disappear for a few weeks and then pop up like a crackhead missing In action. soon after a couple of crazy girlfriends... they would always cheat on him and do dirty shit to him and vice versa and almost causing him to go to jail he got married. he had one child then he got divorce and started to stay away from his only child, If you ask him why he doesn't have anything to do with the child he will say

Its because the child didn't go to college. I find It to be a very weak and poor excuse for you to be mad at your only child because he didn't go to college. I think he stays away from people because he has a lot of skeletons In his closet and one of them Is drug addiction and the other Is hanging out with bad company and very wild and young crazy company. I seen some of his company and the are a bunch of weirdos just like him. he fights with everyone so they can't see his weird actions. most of mommy children are weirdos. the 4th child was Sofia, she was an unusual child she was 5 years younger than me so when she became 10 years old I was 15 and starting to be Interested In boys, when I was hanging with my friends I had to carry her everywhere with me. because mommy didn't expect the two boys to keep her. so I was next In line to be responsible for her. I had to take her everywhere I went, she never said much when she was little so I really can't say much about her as a child. but she did show her true colors at the age of 12 or 13 she was the oldest In the house when my grandmother died and my step grandfather came to live with us. My mother was on a lot of pills and my stepfather was on heroin and my grandfather knew about their drug habit and that's why he was very strict and careful about giving mommy money, because he knew she would use It for drugs and my sister Sofia was terrible to my step grandfather when her and my mother needed money they would wait until he got drunk sitting In his usual chair and as soon as It would turn dark outside Sofia would throw a blanket over his head and dig In his pockets to take his money. one day I came to visit my mother and my grandpa told me this and I ask Sofia who was doing this to grandpa and she told me she was doing this with the twins and I told her to stop this before they hurt him. she said she was doing this to him because he was being cheap with my mother. Sofia was my grandpa's favorite and she treated him like shit. and my grandpa gave Sofia everything she ever needed or wanted. Sofia showed me way back then that she was a thieve. and she was very sneaky and quiet. but when she was about 16 she change and became very loud and obnoxious, she would make fun of people right In their face. she was so sneaky you never knew what she was doing or who she was doing It with. and I didn't like the way she was so wild and had a lot of boyfriends. she would date 3 and 4 guys at the Same time. you never heard anything about her until the guys would start fighting over her. now I know where her daughter's gets this from they have the Same pattern. and jr would fight with the guys because they would spread rumors about her being the neighborhood slut, I remember one guy hit jr In the head with a two by four because the boyfriend beat her up for sleeping with his neighbor. and another time one of her boyfriends broke her jaw because he found her sleeping with his brother. and another time one of her boyfriend lost his mind over her with another guy he climb In her window and caught her In the bed with another guy and cut the guys arm almost off. she had a wild & crazy teenage life. sofia was a quite baby but as a teenager and older women she was Dangerously sneaky & wild. she never had a real marriage she married some guy so he could become a citizen. he found out she was a liar and a thieve then he left her. he was a very nice guy he was going to medical school. than she met this bump that turned Into a crackhead. and she had two daughters from the crackhead and they are just as screwed up as their parents. and I mean they are just as bad In every way... like their mother they are thieves & sluts and now they are worst family member you can Imagine. and now Sam he was mommys last baby from daddy. when Sam was born I didn't see my daddy as much any more back then. at that time mommy worked 2 jobs and she worked until full term with Sam. I remember mommy waking me up In the middle of the night telling me that she's In labor, then she put on her coat waiting for the ambulance to come but they couldn't make It because of the snowstorm the snow was so high. mommy open the door and said to me...I'm going to the corner store so they can help me. I didn't see my mother until the police came to the door to tell me mommy and the baby are or ok. I remember asking the police officer what did mommy have...the officer said you have another brother. and then myself, Carlos, jr, Sofia start to Dance and scream with joy for this new little brother Sam, which I became very attached to. the officer than said that my great grandmother was coming to take care of us kids. all I could do Is say thank you so much. and when mommy brought Sam home I loved him so much that I begged mom to let me stay home from school to help take care of her & baby Sam, mommy agreed because she was very sick after Sams birth. I stayed home so much that I was held back In the fifth grade. but I was happy to stay home and help mommy with Sam, especially because he was very sick too. the doctors told mommy that Sam had a slim chance of survival, because he was sick from liver damage at birth. mommy told me Sam had a fever and she gave him baby aspirin. the doctors told her It was a possibility that Sam had liver damage because he was to young for the baby aspirin. but we were thanking god that he made It. he stayed In the hospital for a couple of months. I was so happy when he came home he was like a little doll. I enjoy helping mommy take care of him and I was only nine years old. and now I had...jr, Sofia & Sam to carry around with me everywhere I went while Carlos runoff and play with his friends. I kept Sam very close to me because he was a very sick baby I guess that's why we've always had a good relationship as we got older. Sam was always quiet when he was a little boy, I always like taking him with me shopping because he help me so much and he was very easy to please. when we gave him gifts for helping... he was so appreciated. I remember my stepfather hit him and shoved him down the stairs In the apartment that my mother live In. and he complained about having a pain In his back, but mommy and the creep stepfather did nothing. they sent him to school the next morning with the pain In his back. and there was a fire drill In school that day he could not walk fast enough to get out of the building so the kids pushed him and knocked him down which lead him going to the hospital with both sides of his hips broken. doctors had to put plates and screws In his hips. when he told me what my stepfather had done to him I told my mother that I promised If my stepfather put his hand on Sam or her again I would kill him. one day he hit my mother and knock her down and she broke her foot... I pick up a long kitchen fork and stabbed him In the arm. he call the police on me but they wind up locking his ass up. after him hitting Sam and my mother I never liked him. Sam always thank me for protecting him from my stepfather. Sam was a sad kid but I always try to make him happy. most of the time I kept him with me until he got older. as he got older I always made sure he had money too because he was always my big helper with everything... he learned how to spend money wisely because I taught him. and I taught him how to become Independent. there's one thing I like about Sam he always came to me for my opinion and he trust my opinion too. as he got old he started to hang around Sofia she showed him all the bad things In life. they started a business together and then him and jr was swindle by Sofia...he learned his lesson and he got away from her. but he had some crazy girl friends as a young man. he had one son they never had a great relationship, I always prayed that It would get better between him and that son, but I know for sure It was because he didn't spend enough time with the kid, because of his crazy girl not wanting anything to do with his kid he would push his son off...on us for the whole summer, and that's why the kid doesn't like him today. I never understood why he would let my sister Sofia babysit for him with that son because her house was crazy. but after a while he started to bring the kid to me every summer for about 5 years because we took great care of that kid. we gave him good summers. but now Sams married and he has another son & this Is his first wife and shes a wonderful person I really like that family. now mommy had the twins...oh my god I don't know what happen to my mother while she was carrying those boys. They were the first children my mother had from my step father, and they were so cute as babies. when they were born everybody would stop me and ask me If they were my children I would say no... and they would ask me where Is my mother? because they saw me with four children all the time and never saw my mother they talked about my mother having so many kids and leaving me to take full responsibility of them. but those twins were so smart at a young age. Dan was the evil twin and Stan was the good twin. when they were babies they were quite but as teenagers everyone got sick of them, they talked so much and most of the time It was about nothing. when the evil twin would do something wrong my stepfather would beat the wrong one and It was Stan taking the ass whipping for that evil Dan, and It still happens today as teenagers Stan gets beat up for Dan. Stan has no children and he's better of because he so cheap. when Stan was young he was one of mom's favorite. but that Dan oh my god mommy did not like him, and why did god give him children?. he so evil he doesn't deserve children. cause he doesn't care about anyone especially me or our mother and I think my mother knew this before she died and that's why she never forgave him. and he got lucky with a very sweet and caring wife. now let's move on to moms newest baby girl she so sweet. her name Is Susan she Is the eighth child she was a darling baby I don't mind carrying her everywhere with me. people love her all over, she was so attached to me I forgot that she wasn't my child. she grew with my daughter, she really showed me that she loved me, she also appreciate anything I did for her as a child. but that didn't last too long because now my life started to change I got married and move out from my mother's house. I didn't move out of the area but

I had less time with Susan because I was working and now my daughter was born so It was less time with my little sister Susan. and now my sister Sofia came back home so Susan start to become attached to Sofia. only now Sofia made Susan do everything at home because Sofia had no time for taking care of all those kids mommy had at home. also Sofia she was lazy when It came to house work. and she had lots of boyfriends she had to chase around...no time for cleaning house, especially cause mommy did have a lot of kids to clean up after. now Susan got stuck with all mommy kids too. Susan wind up having two boys of her own later In life and Sofia was her babysitter, you know Sofia was cuckoo so you can Imagine what she did to Susan's kids. now mommy had given birth to another baby girl Diana number nine I couldn't understand my mother, why Is she having all these children? but I think I do know why because she was the only child and her mother was the only child. and her grandmother could have been the only child, the say she wasn't but we never seen any siblings with great grandma. now Diana was the ninth child that mommy gave birth to. she was very sick complications started because she could not give natural birth due to osteoporosis and spinal problem she had to have cesarean-section with Diana, and I had to take care of her wounds because she started to get osteoporosis and couldn't walk without a cane. this baby was to quiet. anyone that didn't live In my mothers house–Diana thought they were strangers, and Diana never smile I never heard her talk until Diana was about 6 or 7 years old. I never seen her play with the other children, Diana always sat In the corner away from the other kids. I always ask my mother was their anything wrong with Diana? my mother would make jokes about Diana and say there Isn't anything wrong with Diana & mommy would say Diana was a bulshit artist because Diana didn't want to do anything for you so Diana plays like she was slow. but I remember one day Diana came to my house and she said my mother said can she borrow some money? and I was so surprised and I said to her Diana your mother Is my mother and she looked at me with It strange face, she was so confused I never understood It till this day. that's when I start to know she was slow and strange. I thought It was because my mother didn't do anything with these children no recreation at all. I spend a lot of money taking them to parks and recreation and library museum's and buying them toys my mother couldn't afford for them. and I live down the street

2 blocks away from them. Diana heard me call our mother mommy, so what was really going on In her head I was very curious to know but than after that I got pregnant with my 3rd child I was very busy with my own children let alone mommys children. now Diana has two daughters and I hardly even know them, we never had much to talk about when we saw each other. we never had anything In common. when she gathers with the family she's very quiet but behind your back she's sneaky like Sofia. and again Sofia was her babysitter. so you can Imagine what her kids are like too. now I was leaving my first husband and my life was about to change again and I was planning to move but then my mother has another baby number ten, another sweet little girl Karen I was praying that this would be my mother's last baby and It was thank god. this poor baby Karen, she was so cute and she smiled so much. and now there are so many children In my mother's house they don't even know this little baby girl exist. she Is the forgotten child. mommy made sure she was taken care of by letting my stepfathers family take her sometimes. because of mommy being In the wheelchair. when she was 4 years old her father died of a drug overdose. and mommy was left with this baby and 5 other children. times were very hard for these kid with mommy being addicted to pills and their father addicted to heroin, and now he's dead. I never believed that my sisters and brothers would survive this horrible life they had with their parents. now mommy died In the fire and the baby was only 7 years old. i was the most responsible person I knew at that time of mom's death, and I was the only one claiming responsibility for taking care of 6 of mommys children and 3 of my own. so when I look back at all that I have done for 9 children none of them have the right to kick me In the ass. I walked around with my heart In my hands for my family. I wasn't perfect and had a big mouth but I think I was a great person with a big heart.

FAMILY-FAKE-AS-PLASTIC

but I did so much to keep them together after mom's death. I don't want them to kiss my ass. I just want some respect. I know now that I'm done with trying to keep these people together most of them didn't even speak to each other, I stop trying to make them like each other or even like me. there Is no pain like losing you mother, Its 20 years and I still cannot get over this pain. but losing my daughter was just as bad. I think most of you don't know trouble when It knocks on your door but now I do that's why I don't deal with most of you any more. I never had any one to cry to for my lost and my pain. so now I'll take the time off... away from you all to mourn. when you are so busy trying to compete with each other you can not possibly complete what you are supposed to be doing for a prosperous life. I start to see some of my siblings are doing drugs and getting high with their children… that Is one of your biggest problems, and that's why you will do anything for money...you sold your soul to the devil getting high now. and your doing It with you children. I can say for a fact Sofia gets high with her children Tina and betty every day, and that's why you life Is so crazy. It's about that time to check you self because you already wreck yourself and your kids. you need to make sure you have a future because your future looks very dim, I mean this to Tina now she's having a baby and you have nothing but a criminal rap sheet and a welfare check. and now your sister betty who completed school unlike you has a rap sheet with credit card fraud. you girls are to old for you mother to be supporting you. It's really sad that you say you love your mother but you don't even have a job. and you have a husband I wonder what kind of man Stands behind you and watch you live like a thief and a bum? that surely means he's a bum too. your mother owes most of her sibling because she's supporting you old nasty lazy bitches by stealing from us. and you say she's always very sick so why Is she still working? and taking care of your old asses? now the twins... Stan the younger twin.... he never had any children and I think god knew not to give him children because he's a very selfish person. when I was sick and could not work he would come to my house and eat me out of house and home. that cheapskate never brought me a bottle of water. I have never seen him have all or one of his sibling over his house for dinner or a bbq. he will drop by our house unannounced so he didn't have to bring anything. most of the siblings would tell me they don't let him In when he just drops by. and the oldest twin Dan Is the total opposite he will give you the shirt off his back and If he could he will do anything for you but he Is the one everybody hates because he Is very bossy and very opinionated, as soon as he sits In your presence you want to get the hell away from him. he's just annoying. after the family bbqs start to get smaller I started to become sad realizing that we didn't like each other anymore, so I called Sam and we came up with an Idea to get all of our siblings together. Sam said he was going to tell them that I was dying from cancer, I said to Sam I don't think I can go through with this serious and severe lie, but he call all eight of the siblings from mommy side. my phone never stop ringing and I loved It. just to see If they really cared. now I thought wow they loved and cared about me and each other. I thought that we all needed and wanted this time to be together under one roof because we were never all ten under one roof not even In mommys house. It was five of us from my dad and five from my stepfather, when the first older five moved out the last five didn't know much about us. my oldest brother Carlos still today ask me what's the younger siblings names. when the siblings call me they didn't want to tell me that Sam told them I was dying, most of them just told me they were coming to see me but they didn't know Sam and I was cooking up a family reunion. but as always It takes one to be so opinionated and screw up everything we plan.... and that Is Dan the asshole twin. as soon as he called me I knew he was going to throw a monkey wrench In our plans. Dan ask me Is It true... are you sick... do you have cancer? It would never have dawn on him... that I probably don't want to talk about this Issue with having cancer If I had It and thats because hes a straight shooter and sometimes I hate this about him. and so I said no I do not have cancer. I didn't want to lie about having cancer to anyone of them I told Dan, so he said why Is Sam telling all the family that your dying and I said to Dan... Sam and I just need to see all of us together and I thought It was a great Idea because we never seen all of us together. why did I think It was a great Idea? Dan was mad as hell because It was Sam's Idea and he did not want me to agree with anything Sam wanted. but I wanted this to happen just as much as Sam. but Dan was making sure he stop this reunion. only because Dan and Sam had this big fight starting with Dan being to bossy and telling Sam to move to Florida where Dan lives. Dan was not respecting Sam's privacy I told Sam not to move to close to Dan because I know when you live to close to Dan things go bad fast. he lived 30 min from me In ny and he was a pain In the ass, he was so bossy and brags about everything he had. I know him and Sam feel out because he wanted to tell Sam how to live In his house. Dan would tell Sam to buy a bigger house then he needed and how to decorate It, and to buy the car that he think you should have and lets not forget Dan wanted Sam In florida with him because he needed a buddy to brag about being a womanizer...dan was so proud that he had to have Sam around him for that. and when Sam's wife seen the nasty things that Dan did she made sure Sam wasnt around that bulshit life style Dan had. Dan called me telling me to stop the reunion because he could not leave his wife taking care of the children alone. I told him no I'm not stopping this reunion and he said sorry I cannot make It this time, and I said me too I'm sorry you cannot make It but we were all happy he didn't make. and that was the last conversation I ever had with Dan. until one week later jr called me crying ....i ask him what was wrong? he told me that Dan told him he talk to Carlos and Carlos told Dan he was talking to my dad, and my dad started talking about my mother cheating on him with my uncle, his brother.... and he said my dad thinks 4 of her children are probably not his but maybe his brothers children. I called Dan and told him to mind his business and find time for his children, and I told him to stop worrying about who the hell Is our father, he hung the phone up on me and I called him back and ask him why Is he trying to start problems between jr and Carlos and me?... and I said to Dan do you know that jr Is always saying he wants to kill himself...dan said to me that jr Is not thinking Irrational and I said I do believe jr will kill himself because he's on drugs and he's always depressed. this Is upsetting to jr to think his mother could have been dishonest to us about our father for many years. this had been a heavy burden on us for years, but Dan doesn't give a shit... this Is his way to start shit like he always did when he wanted attention. and only now because he miss the reunion...this Is the way he seeks attention making trouble with all of us. I said to Dan you are starting problems and you don't even care about anyone's feelings. and you are mad no one's paying you any attention, then I said to him you have to much time on your hands to be a parent with disabled children. I told him to stay off the phone and stop making unnecessary problems with everyone and take care of your children. I know this made Dan mad as hell, he made a pact with the devil and his keepers are jr and Sofia Tina & betty. now he showed jr how to lie and get an order of protection to keep me and my husband and children out of my own house, I know for a fact that he made jr mad at me because I would not talk to him after he hung up the phone on me. a couple of days after Dan hung up on me, my husband Mike got a call from Dan...he told my husband that jr had a heart attack and I was sitting right next to my husband when he called and I said tell Dan we are going to the hospital to find out what happened to jr. now at this time Im not speaking to Dan because I knew he was causing trouble between me and jr, and I know he's helping jr scheme up something but I never seen this one coming. I tell you Dan you and jr are

REAL SNAKES I MEAN
REAL SNAKES

me and Mike got to the hospital and jr Is sitting up In the bed looking like nothing Is wrong with him, but I didn't jump to conclusions yet. I said to jr what happened? his response Is why are you here? again like he always says to me...but Im always there, and sometimes I'm the only one there. I said I came because Dan called Mike and said you had a heart attack, jr said I'm very sick and I'm not In the mood to talk to you. so I left the room and went to sit In the waiting area. mike came out to the waiting area and ask me If I was ok? and I said to Mike I am not going to go through this with jr because he wants to pick a fight with me. I will wait out here until the doctor comes to tell us what happened to jr. Mike went back In the room to jr and I heard the fuckup jr say to Mike please go home and take your wife with you...he doesnt know I can hear him... now my blood Is starting to boil, I went back Into the room and I see about 20 bottles of pills at the foot of his bed with him, and he's still on the phone talking out loud telling the person on the phone that he had to bring the doctor all the medicine he takes. and he's talking out loud on the phone with Dan. and I said jr I can hear you talking about me and I also said why are you telling my husband to take me home? and then I said Dan called Mike and told us you had a heart attack and we came to find out what happened to you. and now you want me to leave without knowing what happen to you. I said ok I will leave, and then I turned back and I said to him you need a head doctor, and make an appointment for the psychiatrist before you leave this hospital. he said I'm on the phone talking to Dan and he wants to talk to you. I said I do not want to talk to him and jr told me to

33

get out of his life. and then he said you could talk to Carlos but you will not talk to Dan? and I said what the hell does Carlos have to do with this matter right now? now I know jr and Dan didn't want me to associate myself with Carlos and that Is because Dans big mouth. always stirring up shit. like I said they are two evil people. when he told jr that my father was telling Carlos the story…. about my dad not being our dad. Dan doesn't realize what he did to mine and jr relationship…and me and him Dan. but I do believe that mine and jr tightnet relationship probably was never real anyway. because jr did to much to hurt me for me to think he was ever sincere about me. I know now that the two of them did not want me to have anything to do with Carlos because they still hate him from way back and I heard that Dan had a new fight with Carlos, I heard Dan was jealous when Carlos went to visit Susan and a big fight started there with Sam, Carlos, and Susan because evil Dan wanted Susans attention. Dan you all can have each other. again Carlos Is not jr favorite person. now when I left the hospital I told my husband Mike that I will never have anything to do with jr or Dan again after this day In the hospital. I found out later there was nothing wrong with jr. he was a mental case and my mother should have had done something about seeking help for that fool long time ago. but when you're evil It's a different case.

DON'T BITE THE HAND
THAT FEEDS YOU

a couple of months before the big family break up. jr had surgery on his neck and this was right before the family reunion. so I went to the hospital to bring jr back to my house after his surgery so we can take care of him like he did when I had my back surgery. only difference Is that jr brought me back to my house and my daughter-In-law Jade took care of me at that time. now jr had me, Jade, Kirk, Mike to care for him at my house. Stan call me and ask where was I? and I told him that jr had neck surgery than I gave him the hospital address and told him to come see jr. I know Stan was hesitating because Stan and jr hadn't talk to each other because of the ladder he did not bring to jr when he requested to borrow It. but Stan went to see him at the hospital and they had a lot to talk about. and little did I know Stan's wife my sister-in-law...that wants nothing to do with me... works at that Same hospital. she never came up to see neither one of us, and I ask my brother Stan where Is his wife and he told me that she was off and I didnt say anything else. I know If she was there she would not come to that room. now when I got jr to my house It was a big snow storm. the next day my grandsons joe car was buried and my grandson could not get out. jr must have been very high because he went outside and shoveled that car out for joe. I started to scream because I thought he was crazy for shoveling snow after one week of having neck surgery. at that moment I knew he was feeling no pain because of those painkillers. and I start to watch him to see how he was feeling but he was doing better than I thought he would. he went home and started to ride his bicycle like he never had neck surgery and he did a lot of miles on that bike. than he start to act really strange when I came to the house. one day I went there with Jade and Mike, and jr started to scream at me, and I said to him why are you screaming at me? he said because he was naked and I open the door on him, and I screamed back a him and said, I was not entering your apartment down stairs I'm In the upstair apartment so why are you screaming? then I went outside to cool my head because I wanted to tell him off. now I came back In side and I saw a mattress on the floor In the upstair apartment In the bed room, and I ask him where did this mattress come from and he said he does his exercise In that room. and I told him that I need to rent this apartment to Jade. he said oh what happened and I said Jade and Kirk are not getting along with each other, so I have to separate the two of them. so I'm going to rent out this part of the house to Jade. and he looked at me with an angry face and went back down stairs to his apartment. I guess his party was over In the two apartments. if looks could kill. any other time he would always ask me If I needed help... but not this time... I said to my husband he didn't even ask us If we needed help taking Jades things out of the car my hubby look at me and said because he's angry that we are here. he waited In the house a wild and came out after we moved everything already, he try to act like he wasn't mad but I know him...he was heated. now that Jade Is living In the house he thinks shes going to tell me what's going on down stairs with those young boys he's hanging out with In my house. but what he doesn't know Is the neighbors already Informed me about those boys hanging out and getting high with him. they told me that they smell the weed coming from the house. the gas and electric bill was doubling up when he was living there alone. I ask him why are the bills so high he said he didn't know why...but I knew he had someone living there without my permission. because when I go there to pick up the rent from him he's always telling me to call him when I'm close to the house and he will meet me In the front of the house. but one day I didn't call him and I saw a very tall kid come from my house... so I said to Mike who Is the kid coming from our house with the house keys, he was closing and locking the front door. out of nowhere... later he start telling me and Mike the pipes were leaking In his apartment so we called the plumber and electrician. as we prepare to do repair to the house jr refuse to let us In the apartment. every day he's complaining to my son Kirk that the house has so many problems but he will not let us In the down stairs to make repairs.

In my mind I knew he was up to something sneaky...this Is where his scheme starts...but I never expect him to take my house. hey he had a great plan. now I came to the house because my husband wants to talk to him about the repairs and make sure he lets our son In with the plumber. now me and Mike come to the up stairs first to talk to Kirk and Jade and then Kirk knocks on the door with his father and jr lets them In down stairs, and I hear my son and husband Introduce the plumber to jr, now I hear jr say I can't do this right now because I'm sick and I cant take all of these problems and the noise. I went down stairs and said to him what Is your problem? he stood up In front all of us and said you all get out of my house and I said this Is not your house. then I said you are not paying for anything, no rent, no light, no gas and you are telling me to get out of my house. then he screamed the house Is In my name.. and I also screamed at him to call the police and throw us out. he started walking out the door and I followed him to his car, as he got Into his car I told him he will regret fighting with me when he's not paying rent. and the plumber left and said to us I will come back another time because this Is a family problem. and he didn't want to work on the house because he didn't want any problems. me and jr didn't talk again until court 2 years later. this motherfucker jr was making problems with my son Kirk and his girlfriend Jade. still making complaints to them and they were so good to him. they repair the bathroom for $15,000 and repair the plumbing and the electrical problem for $8,000 and they gave him money for gas and tolls for his doctors appointments and food. and he lived down stair for two years without paying me rent. and all that time he never talk to me...but he talk to my husband and children and he keep telling them that he was waiting for his settlement and he's going to pay us everything that he owes us for taking care of him. now Im hearing a year after the repairs were done...he was happy to get It done and paid for by my children, and then throw them out of the house when the work was done. he's a reel low life. he start to make lies about the house being In foreclosure but this was his way to trick his nieces and sister to help him with his scheme to get my kids out and lie and tell her she's In. he lied to the evil nieces Tina and betty and that thief sister Sofia and told them that we were not paying him for the house. and they believed him and they ran with the scheme so they would have a place to live because they just got evicted out of Susan apartment. now they started to harass Jade at her job by sending a strange man to give her a fake eviction. they scared Jade till she had to call the police about a strange man chasing her at her job. jr Is at the house every thursday with Tina harassing Jade and Kirk by turning off the electricity when they are at work. and they would make her food go spoil. now when Jade calls the police the bitch Tina Is speaking to the police telling them that (we) meaning her and jr are trying to evict Jade and Kirk. can you Imagine this bitch Tina that don't have shit… and they are trying to throw my children out of their own house. because her homeless ass needs to have somewhere to live with her bum husband and bum sister and bum mother and soon to be her unfortunate baby. born to fucked up parents and fucked grandparents who steal from others. they have too much nerve but no fuckin money and no fuckin jobs. those bitch are trying me so hard and they know we have more to lose then they do. and that's why they are so bold to help the asshole jr. they tried so bad to live In my house but Its not going to work. they are desperados. and I'm going to make sure they get what they deserve and It ain't my house. when jr and Tina started too harass Jade they took time to make Jade so upset that she would move. they threw dirt on her car and they came to the door every thursday to harass her with a fake eviction notice 3 times. and then jr and Tina came with a real eviction notice. now I'm sure jr remembers that day and I hope he never forgets It. because he came up stairs while Kirk and Jade was moving out and told Kirk that he wasn't supposed to be In his house. I know now after they moved that jr came up stairs to threatened my son, and I know jr has a gun because Sam told me he gave jr a gun many years ago. I kept telling my son not to be at the house when jr Is there. because I never trust that motherfucker any more especially after me my husband and my son and daughter In law all housed him feed him and care for him. and now he's In court with us every month for a lie he made up to get this house. one night 10:30pm we are about to go to sleep when the sheriff knocked on my door and said we have an order of protection for jr. and I couldn't believe my ears. he made this lie up so he can get us out of the house, he's living very good buy taking the shortcut and that's lying and cheating his way through life. the first day we went to court, me and Mike went to the house to pick up Kirk and Jade. Kirk was coming back from a haircut and that's when we saw jr and Tina coming up the block driving his new car leaning to the side like a thug. then he drives side by side and block us In and starts to stare at us saying nothing. I screamed at Mike and told him to drive away from him before he lies and say we did something to him. then we told Kirk not to park there because we were afraid that he would do something to Kirks car. so Kirk followed us to the court. that day jr act like he was afraid of us he was not. oh and he was In the car with out his neck brace, but when he came In the court he act like he was In pain with the neck brace on. and walking with a cane and the bitch Tina acting like she was helping him by carrying his paperwork. which I believe was nothing but doctors letters to say he had a neck surgery. he doesn't have any receipts to say he paid for anything because he didn't pay for shit. but there's nothing wrong with him now. and that Is what I know for a fact because I seen him shoveling snow and riding bikes. but someday someone will catch him lying and faking being disabled very soon.

BACK STABBERS

once In the court room the judge ask Mike, Kirk, and me did we know why we were there In court today? and we said no we did not. then the judge start to read the charges against us. I told the judge this was all lies my brother made to steal my house. and that we were In the wrong court and we should be In real estate court. then the judge ask jr could he work this family matter out without the courts? and jr said no... because I'm mad and I'm sick and they don't understand Im very sick. and the judge ask him did you talk to your sister? and he said no I didn't. the judge also ask jr are you sure you can't handle this matter without wasting taxpayers money for something that you can work out with your sister? he start to Stand up... out of his chair and act like he was In so much pain with his back. the judge ask jr If she should adjourn the case because he's not feeling well? and then she ask him why didn't you stay home and postpone this for another day? he told her... he's only In pain because he cannot sit In those hard chairs In the courtroom. and then the snake start to rub his back all over the wall. he look so fake, he was really putting on a show. and I know the judge knew It too. I know he just drove from queens where he lives to the Bronx to pick Tina up. and back to queens to court, and then back to the Bronx to drop Tina off. and back to queens where he lives. and he did this for the 5 times that we went to court. back and forth was 10 trips to the Bronx and back to pick up his lying witness Tina. you know If he had a bad back there's no way In hell he would be able to make all those trips... fake ass liar. I still can't believe how he went all the way to the Bronx just to pick up a liar for his scam, and just think the way he use to say he hated Tina... It's unbelievable how he used her too. but she will not believe It until he's finished using her. as soon as I had the chance I let the judge know It too. the judge then ask all of us Individually did we need an attorney? and we all said no we do not. then she said ok she told jr to present his case and she told him to call his first witness and the jerk call me. the judge stopped him and ordered all of us to seek attorneys. then she call the jerk jr Incompetent, and told him to stop while she gets him an attorney. the case was adjourned again. I also ask the judge to please give us more time for my husband to have shoulder surgery and she gave us the time. now at this time my husband had shoulder surgery and I had enough time to get all of my evidence against jr. while waiting for the third court appointment, I got pictures that the bitch Tina posted on facebook with him everywhere without his neck brace. and pictures of him shoveling snow and doing thug poses... bending down with no problem. and at parties and restaurants with the bitch and no brace on. now that we are back In court wasting taxpayers money with this weirdo, for the third time In court the judge ask me why didn't I get an attorney I told her I didn't need one...because Im going to tell the truth. and she said ok. and I started the case very well with lots of proof that jr was a liar and a thief. when the judge told me to start the case and ask him the 1st question, I ask why did It take you 2 years to bring us to court for an fake assault case? he said at first he didn't want to do It to us and that's because he was trying to figure out how to make this lie look good. And he said because he was sick of me. then I ask him why does he come to court with his neck brace, when he never wear It anywhere else? and he said I can wear It anytime I want too... and rolled his eyes and sucked his teeth like a little girl. the judge told him not to answer me like that. then she said ask him another question, I ask him why are you angry with me and why did you bring me to court? he said I'm sick of you and you mouth. the judge told him again not to answer me like that. then she said ask him another question. I ask him Isn't It true you owe me back rent? and I will you are trying not to pay me from 2014 to 2017? he said you are a liar because I gave you $2,700 for rent. and I said how can you give me $2,700 when you said you had no Income? and he said that was how you arrange It, he also said that's how you always do things...you arrange things your way. and I said... didn't you promise to pay us all the rent you owed us? and Isn't It true you said you were waiting for a disability settlement? he said that's what I gave you. and I ask him do have proof of what you said you paid me? and he said no. and I told the judge I have proof that he paid me $600 a month for rent and I have the receipts. and I paid $1,200 for mortgage and $800 for utility bills and I have receipts to prove It. the judge told me to ask him another question before we adjourn to lunch. I pulled out 6 pictures of him all over the Bronx and queens and Manhattan without his neck brace doing all kinds of poses with no back or neck problem. I ask him Is this you? and where Is your neck brace? his eyes start to cross and he stood up and leaned over trying to get a closer look to see where and how I got those pictures. and then he scream out that's Illegal and he also said someone needs to take those pictures from her. and the judge ask me where did I get those picture from? and I said they are perfectly legal because I got them from facebook and twitter. and the judge said yes she's right they are legal. and then she order all of us out off the court room until lunch. now when we all start to leave the courtroom I hear jr's attorney ask him...do you have those receipts? and jr said yes and he said are talking about the ones from now? and his attorney said no the ones that your sister says she has. and he said no… his attorney said you better get them. as we left the courtroom, I walked over to Tina with my receipts and told her she's helping him for nothing, because I have all my receipts to show he did not pay for shit. when I started telling her she will never get the chance to live In my house she said auntie I didn't want to live In your house. I said then why are you here fully pregnant and ready to give birth In this court for a fucked up liar and thief? and then I felt Kirk pulling me away from her saying don't talk to her. then Tina said Kirk why are you screaming at me? and he said because you are a mother fucker helping that punk steal from my parents. and she started to cry and again I said to Tina why are you here? while Kirk Is pulling me away...and I said why don't you go find your husband and enjoy your baby? she said she didn't know what was going on, but I knew she was a liar. because she told my son one day that I'm spreading dirty rumors about her mother's health, which are not dirty rumors Its the truth. she's always telling us that we don't do anything for her mother when she sick. but her mother wants It to be kept a secret when she sick so what the hell can we do? when Its a big fuckin secret. and she told my son I never did anything for her. she's right I never did anything for her because she's at my house stealing any and everything she can get from me. back at the court, I ask Kirk to stop pulling me and I told his father to take him out of the court. because now I hear a lot of noise and keys and I turned around and we were surrounded by court clerks. they told Kirk to leave the court and they ask me what happen? and I told them that my brother owed me $320,000 and we were trying to prove our case but my son got up set. and now I turned around and I see the judge Standing there with her sandwich In her hand watching the whole thing with us unfold outside the courtroom. and just before we exit the courtroom the judge said to us do not go outside this courtroom and start any arguments between you all. now because of Kirk pulling me and the judge seen this she adjourned the case. but thank god that she did because all hell was braking lose that day, and jr was pulling the bitch Tina away from me. telling me not to talk to her. and I know why he didn't want me to show her my receipts proof that he didn't pay for my house. now weeks later we return to court and I notice that jr and Tina are not In court. we go In to see the judge and she said the case would be adjourned again because jr's attorney Is sick. but right after she said that she said to Kirk that he almost caused himself to go to jail and she said she saw him pulling his mother. than she told him to apologize to his parents and the day was over again another time to come back to court. I know my son was sorry for pulling me and I know why he's so angry about this 3rd or 4th court adjournment and this whole family feud. my son almost lost his job because of this bulshit lie with this screwed up person my mother gave me called a brother, and that screwed up brother Is so wrong for lying on my son to get him lock up. my son took great care of jr he's going to be so sorry for treating my son so bad. because he was a great person to his uncle. and that was my favorite brother and he turn on us like a snake. i will never forgive that fucked up brother never. now weeks go by before we return to court. this time In court we see the evil bitch Tina Is not with jr. maybe she finally got the message that jr Is using her or she went to give birth and has no more time to start any more chaos In our lives. and now he's walking In the court just fine without his neck brace or cane or suitcase. we look at each other and I rolled my eyes and said to my daughter as we enter the court here comes the dog that use to be your favorite uncle. he turn to see who I was talking to and he realize Its my daughter, the one he hasn't seen In 2 or more years. the one that would have done anything for him....but he's telling the judge that he wants an order of protection against her. he had people going to her house to serve her a subpoena to get an order of protection, because she told him that he should stop crying about what her mother didn't do for him and thank her for taking care of his old ass for so long. he's really a punk. Ana ask him what's wrong are you mad because my mother paid your rent and utility bills but not your car note. so he was afraid of Ana because she said that to him. he's a real punk. now that he sees my daughter Ana In court I know he's afraid. my daughter didn't do a damn thing to hurt him and she just told him off one time for starting an argument with her brother. you see when Kirk was In the house he heard jr and Dan and Diana talking to each other on a three way phone call very loud. and they were telling each other how fucked up and tricky I was, and saying how much they hated me. my son said he heard all three of them talking about me loud and clear as If they were all In the house with him. til this day I think jr was trying to get Kirk out of the house by making Kirk mad and then he would call the police on my son several times to make a fake case against him. so I know when he told jr off jr planned this. that's when Kirk went down stairs and told them to stop talking about his mother. than he told them my mother did a lot for you and those other sisters and brothers you are talking to. but jr lied and said he's not talking bad about his mother. he said It was Dan and Diana talking bad about your mother. that's jr always blaming someone else. and after that conversation we all wind up In court with jr's lies. back to that day In court, we all went up stairs to the courtroom and the court clerk called all of us In the court now the judge ask jr's attorney did they serve my daughter Ana? the attorney responded no your honor we could not reach her. that's when my daughter came out and said I'm here your honor. and the judge said ok Ms Ana but you do not have to be here... but you can stay for moral support for your mom. and the judge told her she was dismissed because they did not serve her. oh my god… jr looked like he wanted to die. jr open his pocket book and yes I mean pocket book and said your honor I have another charge on my nephew. and judge told him to keep his paperwork and she also said I'm sick and tired of this family she said I don't want to hear anything about this case with that house. I was saying thank god because we are In this court for an order of protection not a real estate matter. and that's just what she said. than I said ok what about the money jr owes me and the judge said do you have any proof that he said he owes you any money? and I said yes I do. I went to get the paperwork out of my bag that says. my sister and my nephew are paying the sum of $1,200 for the mortgage and jr signed It In 2008. and the judge said please pass that document up here to me. she looked It over and said the document has your signature on It Mr jr and she said I'm sure It matches your signature because Im comparing It to the other document that I have here. and the judge told jr's attorney to show his client the document. the attorney stated that the document may not be authentic. then he passed It to jr and the judge ask jr did you sign that document? jr answer I my have. that's when the judge said this document was sign In 2008 and I don't think Ms Judy Is going to fraudulently bring a document with his signature from 2008 and Its now 2017. then jr's attorney said objection your honor...this Is Irrelevant to this case and then the judge said no this proves that he owes the defendant money. now the judge started to become angry and she told me not to mention anything else pertaining to the house. and I started to cry. now she ask me do I have any more question about the allegation that my brother said happen to him In the house? and I cried out loud and said no your honor I just want this case to be over. the judge than ask the attorney what does your client want from this court. and that attorney ask the judge for a 2 year order of protection the judge told him no I will give him a 6 month order of protection against Ms Judy and a 6 month order of protection against Mr Kirk and no order against Mr Mike. then the judge order the case Is close. I saw that fat bastard sitting outside the courtroom waiting to see If we would leave first and I look at him and I said I'm not finished with your ass. and you can believe he robbed me but he will not get away with It. I'm going to the next court to sue him for my house back or my $320,000.

CUT THE FAMILY TREE

there was a time when you could not keep me from my family...so-call brothers and sisters. but now when someone ask me, am I having a mother's day bbq or thanksgiving dinner with my family? I say yes and I add to that... and It's only with my children, and my cousins and that's my only family. no more brothers and sisters the tree was cut down November 2016. and now my roots from my mother's side was dug out July 2017 when that bastard jr throw my children out of my house that I was paying for since 1996. and then while my daughter-In-law and son are moving out of the house with the help of my grandson... without bothering jr... he came up stairs from the basement and walked around to the front of the house... walk up In the house without knocking on the door... just walked right up to my son's face and said to my son... that my son was trespassing. and then he push himself close to my son face and said you don't listen do you? and that's when my grandson had to video tape him to stop him from attacking my son. and my daughter-in-law had to call the police to tell them what he did, because jr would have lied and say my son attacked him. but this could have turned out worse then him lying about Kirk. Kirk could have beat the hell out of jr, and that's what he was probably waiting to see If Kirk was going to attack him, so he could shoot my son with that gun Sam says jr has. and It would have happened In front of my grandson and daughter-in-law. thank god my son kept calm. believe me jr Is a lucky fuck because I would have killed jr If anything happen to my son. jr better watch out for what he does to my children. I know jr would never kill for his child because he doesn't even talk to his own child and he's the only child jr has. his only child and he treats him like shit. I do understand well If that child hated his father jr. I know that the bitch Tina called my daughter one day telling her to leave her auntie Diana alone, and my daughter was going to break her nose for sticking It In our business. you see when you talk about Tina's mother she wants to kill you. but when she talked bad about me to my daughter she never expected to hear my daughter defending me. Tina got a call from Diana saying that my daughter Ana called her and cursed her out, but Diana knows why my Ana cursed her out. It was because she was on the three way phone conversation with jr and Dan talking shit about me. when my son told my daughter my daughter call that bitch Diana and told her off she couldn't take the heat. Diana cant Stand up for herself when she gets caught talking lies about me. so she calls Tina thinking Tina can scare my daughter. no way... when Tina call my daughter my daughter told Tina off so bad she said to my daughter shut up and go fight with your mother. I know my niece Is sorry she said that to my daughter because she's going to get her ass whipped If my daughter catch her. Tina knows she just woke up a sleeping lion. now I see things on facebook I don't like. my so called oldest son who never gave a shit about me or his sister or his brother.

LETTING GO OF TOXIC FAMILY MEMBERS

I was so surprised to see a couple of things on face book. my sister Susan was getting married and I could not attend the wedding. my youngest child was going through a terrible time In his life and he needed me to be here for him. and I was going through some financial difficulty. I could not come to the wedding without at least a wedding gift. that would have cost me about $300 to $500 and a plane ticket round trip for me and my husband and hotel stay would have been about $3,000 and time from our jobs which we could not get because we didn't have the free time like Sam and Sofia has. and Sofia doesn't have a house that she has to pay mortgages for. remember she's the one that lives any and everywhere. that's one of the reasons you and her had that fall out, not paying you rent. and Sam and his wife make great money they also live close to you so It didn't cost them much at all to drive to you. and If you had your favorite sister and your favorite brother stay at your house Im sure I would have to stay In a hotel. because you don't even have a house you have an apartment. and I'm not the only one that didn't come, what happened to the other 7 brothers and sisters? you don't like them neither I guess not because you didn't just hurt me you hurt other sibling too, by your facebook statement to us...for the world to see, but maybe you already know this and just don't care. If thats so you are not the person I used to know as a loving little sister. then your are just like the other siblings a grown piece shit. and this was the time that the no good brother jr was living In my house and claiming that he was waiting for his compensation disability case to go through. and he said he didn't have an Income so he couldn't pay me $ 600 a month for his rent. can you Imagine he live In my house two years without paying me rent. and then when his settlement did come he took an order of protection out on me my husband & my kids just to get us out of the house we were paying for.. so I was very apologetic to my sister but I guess It didn't mean anything to her because she made a statement on facebook that broke my heart. she said thank you so much to my [favorite brother Sam & favorite sister Sofia] for making It to my wedding and always being there when I need you. ok Susan we know Sofia Is your favorite sister because she took care of your children while you worked and went to school. but when you needed me I was there to especially when mommy died. I guess that meant nothing compare to Sofia taking care of your kids. and you two were always very close anyway. you also remember she left you In a terrible debt, owing a lot of money for that apartment you left her and her daughters In, and they didn't pay for living there neither. than she allowed her daughters to call you out on facebook saying you were an unfit mother because you didn't do anything for your son that they screwed up. remember that favorite sister of yours was smoking weed and drinking with your 14 year old son and her own children. and you had to detox your 20 year old son and show him how to live a good life without drugs that your favorite sister poisoned your child with. so I don't understand how she was your favorite sister but I guess you know why. and your favorite brother I never knew that Sam was your favorite brother after all I ever seen was him beating you up. and the last time we were all together he bustered your mouth and broke you tooth with a wooden shoe all because he demand you stop cursing. and you were a grown women. your husband could have broke his jaw. and before that when you and your favorite brother lived with me when mommy died you two never got along because he gave you a black eye he said because you talked back to him. but again you are very forgiving to what they do to you. I never understood how you forgive them and forget me. I did nothing wrong to you I guess that I have to do something wrong to you to get on your favorite list.

CUTTING THE CORD OF THE MIDDLE CHILD

now my oldest son the middle child talking bad about me and his siblings. And all on Facebook with your dum new girl. And this Is what you always do when you get a new girlfriend show off and act like a bad boy. Then after you leave them you want to come running back In mine and your sister life. But this Is It I had enough of your stupid bad boy ways. the way you treat us bad because you have a new crazy girl. You and all those crazy girl friend can have each other Im done. the way I see It, he never liked or care for us ever. I never felt so uncomfortable sleeping In the Same house with him when he was angry. he treats us like we are strangers. and he talks to us like he doesn't know us. and we are his only family. and I could not understand him, I really think he has an anger Issue and when he gets mad he doesn't care about anyone. I us to think he care more for his friends but when he gets mad at them he doesn't care what he does to them neither. I remember he was mad at one of his best friends and he hit him In the head with a bottle and crack his friends head. and his friend did not have him lock up or beat him up. and no one really knew til today what was the reason he hit his best friend In the head with the bottle? I know why he did It because that friend Is the one that's going to tell everybody he crack his head with a bottle so don't fuck with him. That makes him look like a bad boy. But that friend should have sued his ass. and his friend did not threatened him. That son of mine just wanted people to think he's a thug. because that friend was a humble person. I know the kid very well. this Is not shocking because when he was 16 he always wanted to be a thug, and wanted everyone to think he was a badass rapper. And cutting classes In school to get high with his friends. and he wanted me to buy him expensive fancy thug clothing for school, one day he wanted a $600 jacket and a pair of Jordan sneakers and when I told him no, he took a bat and broke the tv In his room. and when I entered his room to see what he broke, he told me to get the hell out of his room before he knocks my head off. then I called the police, once he knew I was calling them he try to leave before they came, I lock him In the house and he drop the bat and picked up the hedge cutters and started breaking down the door to get out. and I was blocking the door with my body and he scream at me to move out his way or else he would knock me out of the way. thank god the police came In time to lock him up. after that I put him In a group home for troubled boys. he was suppose to return home after one year. but I didn't take him back In my home because I didn't believe that he would not act crazy after one year. because he was still angry and fighting In the group home. so he went to live with his sister. the group home was sending him to her with a check for a bed and other things that he would need to live with her. but he wanted to take the check and get high with his friends again. now his sister and him got Into a fight about the check and he attacked her, than cut her with a knife, now the police came and locked him up again Than he wind up coming back home to me again. but he was back on the streets with his friends getting high and now not working. then I told him I was going to put him out again, and he started to listen to my rules again and he got a job. my best friend got him a great job with her husband and after 6 months he got fired. because he was waking up late for work every day. he was out all night getting high with his friends again. getting high always meant more to him than anything Important. then I told him to go try job corp. and he went up state to job corp and finished his program and came back down to live with me again. but he came back with this crazy girl friend and they thought that I was going to let them live with me. but I did not like that rude girl. I remember when I first met her, she came to my house with my son and she was walking straight to his bedroom without speaking or looking at me. but I stop her and said to her before you come through my house you should at least say hello to me. and she said she didn't see my big ass sitting right In front of her. I told my son shes rude and do not bring her back here In my house again. he stay with her for 10 years and they gave each other hell. he's my oldest son who never came to see me while I was In the hospital having back surgery. but he was at that Same girlfriends mothers bedside every weekend when that women was In the hospital for Infections and abscesses from heroin addiction. and having surgery from working hard driving taxi and trucks and buses for a living. And he never bothered to take time to come see me In the hospital ever. that girl friend he claimed put him through a lot of shit and left him with nothing. he call me one day and ask me how was I doing and I told him I needed back surgery and he said ok mommy I'm going to come see you before you have the surgery. I went to surgery and that oldest son of mind never came one day to see me In the hospital or at home. he called me and said that his girl friends mother Is very sick. and I ask him what Is wrong with her? and he told me she may need to have her leg amputated. but she was blessed It never happen. so I ask him again when am I going to see you? and the next thing he said he doesn't have a car and that I lived very far from him, I told him ok Its alright I forgive him. but I was really upset because that kid never showed me that he loved me or cared for me. I didn't see him for two years. so one day he called me and he ask me to come from long Island to the bronx to help him move. 6 months after my back surgery. because he caught the girl cheating on him. and he chopped up all the furniture In the apartment with a machete. when I brought him back to my house he was so cold to me. one day I needed water In the house I ask him to please go to the store to buy bottled water and I told him I will give him the money and my car. he told me that he felt like a slave to me, I laughed at him he has never never done anything for me. I told him that his brother always shop for me but he was at work at the time and I couldn't carry the water. I was telling him that he's lazy and careless. than he ask me can he borrow my car to go to queens to be with his friends. I told him no because the last time I gave him my car he was all over searching for the person or persons who killed his friend. now mind you he doesn't know a damn thing about this kid, he only went to school with the kid years ago. this was a friend of a friend. and I told him another thing you brought my car back with weed all on the back seat and floor. I don't smoke so I didn't want that shit In my car. he's so busy getting high from the weed that he doesn't have time to clean my car or do anything for me. only time for his friends. where are his friends when he needed help with food and a home, and when he didn't have a dental plan. I paid for him to get his wisdom tooth out of his mouth for $1,000 just to not see him In pain. And your a grown adult with no medical Insurance, but he never gave a shit what I felt. and I gave him everything he ever needed or wanted as a child until he was 18 years old, I look at his Christmas pictures and said I wished I had a mother like me. and that's the Same thing that his ex-girlfriend use to tell him. and he use to bragg to her about everything I gave him when he was a child. his father never gave him a dam dime or time. his stepfather my husband gave him everything since he was a year old. so I guess he's mad at me for his real father not being In his life. when his real father start smoking crack I was pregnant with him I left his father to save our life. and married a good man that raised him as If he was his own child. and that man gave him everything as a child. and If you didn't get anything from us as an adult and your brother and sister did that's because he treated us like shit. and you are still treating us like shit. and you have a new girlfriend whos Insane just like you. he always dating girls with junkie parents. and where does he find these people the bronx. If this Is the case he needs to screen these women background and vice versa. both of you hate your mother's. so I guess thats what these two have In common together not loving their mothers but I not a junkie. I guess the two of you sit up all night talking about how you hate your mother's. and now you too have company to share your sad lies about your childhood being so bad. your jobs over looked you with bipolar and multiple personality. maybe one day one of you will realize that you need to go have a psychological test for at least one of you before destruction. because one of you will erupt. and I don't know Ms coco well but I know she's not coco shes cuckoo. one thing I do know and that Is my son has bipolar and multiple personality. and are you the first one outside of us who Is going to see that Dangerous side of him. believe me girl you better be careful when he erupts because you may think your a crazy ass but he's crazier than you. and you are so disgraceful with your mouth. you and your new girlfriend took money from your sister and when she ask for It back you told your sister to suck your penis. do your girlfriend think that you respect her when you say nasty things like this to your sister. all you do Is give her sex cause you don't respect her. and that's all you do for her she will see. I remember you told me and your sister that you was so happy she didn't have any children from you because she's crazy. are you making sure she doesn't have any children from you? because she's always talking about your baby with her. she should make sure she doesn't have any from you too. two Insane people that stays on facebook telling the world how they spend their life all day every day need lots of professional help not the people on facebook. and I know that you do not respect her and one day she will wake up and see the wicked person you really are. and I see the problem... Its you... not me. If you don't respect your mother or your sister the only two women In your life and we didn't do anything wrong to you but show you right from wrong, you will never be bless. you may think you are bless with that girl you are not. she told me that she didn't like her own mother the very first time I met her. If she had problems with her mother she should not feel free to tell me this the first day she met me. she didn't know me at all, that's why she's not bless. but I know she's like you with that. because people are always telling me you told them you hate me. and after all these years I don't know why. just tell me In my face and not through other people or facebook. that goes to show you that both of you have some Issue that your mothers can not fix. both of you need god and a mental doctor. and I know god would never except your ways so I will not neither. I'm the one who gave you life but god will take It If you don't deserve to be here on this wonderful earth. when you call the police on your brother because he told you not to disrespect you mother and sister you were wrong not him. that's why no one with any sense deals with you. and I see on facebook that you have the bad family members as your audience. you keep pleasing those kind of people they have no jobs they steal from everyone they know and they steal from the government too. and If that's your loving family then Im blessed to be away from you and them. they hated your mother just because I don't get high with them and I didnt take part In their criminal activities. your new girlfriend was only with you for one year when you start to fight with your sister and she didn't tell you to stop. she made the fight bigger than what It was because she wanted you all to herself. and that showed me that she's very selfish. and she allowed you to talk disrespectful to me without stopping you. and I did nothing wrong to her and she went on facebook and said I was an unfit mother she Isn't a mother and she will never be anyone's mother but to her dog. so she can't say whos an unfit mother because she doesn't know me with her selfish ass. I hope her dog has puppies. so If she shares you with her family [the puppies] then maybe I'm wrong. because maybe she just doesn't like your family. god bless you any way you take It with her and not us. everyone knows when they are wrong eventually you will too.

THIS IS NOT SEE YOU LATER THIS IS GOODBYE

I am no longer in your lives to force you to like each other. and you don't have to pretend In my presence that you like me anymore. I was the one you all always said was crazy. did you all look at your own life and say to yourselves that you are all just as crazy as me, as a matter of fact some of you had more crazy shit In your life than me. thats why Im not saying see you later anymore Im saying goodbye, cause some of you are crazy as hell. jr Is the reason why all of this Is going on. even though he doesnt think he has anything to do with this family war. from the last family bbq jr open the gates to hell. so now he's jealous that he's not my favorite brother anymore because now he started a war. once jr never liked Carlos or Stan or Sam Sofia or Susan and Dan never like Carlos and Dan and Sofia and Sam never like Stan and Stan never like Susan Karen and Tina never like john and betty never john Tina never like Dan and Stan and Sam and Karen Susan. poor little me I really don't know or care who don't like each other anymore Im done. they all called me crazy the should really look In the mirror. Carlos had a couple of crazy women too. that's why he has kids all over the place. and thank god that crazy life Is over for him because he would have been like my mother and father kids all everywhere. he now married to a wonderful women Natasha who Is one of my favorite sister-in-law with a beautiful daughter. and then there's the jackass jr who had one crazy ex-wife Emma, I say shes so crazy for hooking up with my brother, and then she had a son john. I was always wondering how they called me crazy when these two people were crazy as hell. I feel sorry for their son john his mother was lucky to get away from my brother and I will never understand how she had a child with this junkie and liar and thief. not to say she gave him his only child and he treats him like the child never exist. this cruel brother told his son that he doesn't want anything to do with him or his grandchild, this cruel jr even told some family members that this wasn't his grandchild. he Is going to hell for the things he said about an Innocent baby. and his son did nothing wrong to deserve for his father to say mean thing like this. don't worry john your father Is living In hell with himself. and he's digging his own self deeper Into hell. and his best friend Dan jr partner In crime. and the quiet sneaky rob you In your face Sofia, looks sweet but will fuck you life up bad. and she had 2 daughters just like her fucked up bad ass bitches. I never knew anyone worse than the oldest one she's a loud ugly sneaky thief and the way she smiles In your face and offers to help you would fool you with her kindness just like her mother. the are like palm reading gypsies, and her mother my sister Is her twin and the younger daughter Is the sneaky quiet storm like her, and she will Stand back and watch the fire burn but you will never see that she started the fire. once you see these three people try to enter you life run fast, because they will charm their way Into you life and fuck you up bad. that sister Sofia really sleep with the devil, because those daughters father Is just as fuck up as my sister. now Dan I know now what I never Imagine about this brother he was blessed with a wonderful wife. but she was cursed with a deceiving slut and a conspirator. my mother told me she would never forgive him for giving her so much trouble but I never knew he would be worst as an adult he has the mind of the devil and he's proved that to me. especially when he can't use you. he will ruin your life anyway he can. I guess I will die and never forgive him like my mother. he has a couple of children and he acts like hes a single man with a lot of bitch time and that means making problem with everybody. and his twin Stan I know he says he's a man of god but he's a liar too and a punk. he call me one day and told me to stay away from his house because Im happily married and he doesn't want his wife to know about his crazy family. and his junkie parents. we stay away from him and later he came back Into our life for a couple of years he came to spend time with my husband and never had much to say to me and I never met his wife until our aunties funeral. and they never associated or Invited us over their house. but since the last bbq jr told Stan something but Stan did not tell us what jr said In completion.

all Stan said Is that jr told him I said he was cheap. and I told Stan yes I did say that and I never hid It. I said It to his face. so what was the real reason that Stan stop coming to see me and my husband oops I mean come to see my husband. Is It because jr try to make everyone hate me and It's because of him stealing my house yes. til today Stan has not come to my face and say why he's staying away from me. all's well ends well don't have to feed his cheap ass anymore. and I hope god gives him some children maybe he will learn to stop being so cheap and selfish. and Sam Sam Sam Sam I don't know what to say about you. once upon a time you were my favorite brother too. and your wife Is still one of my favorite sister-In-laws, but you start to stick your nose In something you knew nothing about. I try to explain to you the way your brother was scamming me out of my house and how he was living there rent free for 2 years not paying me and disrespecting me. and took a fake order of protection on us. you didn't seem to care. I was hoping that you would call me and say sorry to me but you didn't I'm still waiting. maybe you are just staying clear of all the family bulshit thats fine but you still need to know what you did wrong. you just told me to get my son out of my house so jr can have peace. but It doesn't work like that. jr doesn't deserve peace because he didn't pay for peace. you have to pay where you sleep he didn't. you had a son that you didn't have a good relationship with. I didn't tell you what to do with that child. but I'm not going to tell you that all the good times we had together you must have forgot. but It's ok. because I know I didn't do anything wrong to you so I don't know why you told me what to do with my son. you never seen my receipts so until you remember the good person that I was always to you and your brother I have nothing more to say. and now the twins, the hell with you the oldest one Dan will go straight to hell none stop. just like you put me through hell you will get It back. and I feel so sorry for his loving wife and kids because they would be much happier In life without him. and the other half of you there's no words for you but [follower] [simple] and still looking for a mother. as old as you are. you are the real forrest gump and thank god you don't have kids stick with the dogs. and Susan you always called me crazy but you are more crazy than me. remember you let your sister Sofia babysit your kids and thank god they are doing ok now but your sister screwed your oldest child up with smoking weed and you know her and her daughters messed your son up bad. and you trust her with you life and I mean your kids are your life. so you know that I would not leave my dog with Sofia let alone my kids and I damn sure would not leave her living In my house. we know how Sofia pays rent she doesn't. so I think you are more crazy than me. and Diana you talk so much shit about me and you called me crazy also but you had 2 children and we still don't know who or how anybody slept with you. your children walk pass their fatherssssss every day and they don't even know them. I know my mother gave birth to you but I feel that I really don't know you. so I'm out of words for you but one dingbat. and Karen you are suppose to be on my side. but you need to know that hate Is strong and when someone tells facebook that they hate your sister you should not say thats funny. you should find out why and the truth. I hope you are not In the need for friends. because you look like a snake, I see you laughing with the old dum ugly girl my son Is fucking. you know I'm not on facebook telling the world my life. not telling people that I hate them on facebook Im telling them In their face. and you have two children that I love and they love me. not because I'm a dirty bitch but because I'm a loving sister and auntie. I hope that you told them the truth about why I don't have anything to do with you and no more happy bbqs, its because you are laughing with bitches that do dirty shit to your sister. I hope you are happy with your new friend. looks like It your dressing alike. careful trying to be friends with the devil. and you fucked up not me. I see you. all of you thats why I don't see you later anymore It goodbye mother fuckers.

Printed in the United States
By Bookmasters